Máq
simples

por Becky Gold

Scott Foresman
is an imprint of

PEARSON

Glenview, Illinois • Boston, Massachusetts • Chandler, Arizona
Upper Saddle River, New Jersey

Photographs

Every effort has been made to secure permission and provide appropriate credit for photographic material. The publisher deeply regrets any omission and pledges to correct errors called to its attention in subsequent editions.

Unless otherwise acknowledged, all photographs are the property of Pearson Education, Inc.

Photo locators denoted as follows: Top (T), Center (C), Bottom (B), Left (L), Right (R), Background (Bkgd)

Opener: ©Jim Craigmyle/Corbis
1 Jupiter Images
3 ©Jim Craigmyle/Corbis
4 (Inset, C) ©Jim Craigmyle/Corbis
5 Andy Crawford/©DK Images
6 Jupiter Images
7 Andy Crawford/©DK Images
8 Clive Streeter/©DK Images

ISBN 13: 978-0-328-47441-7
ISBN 10: 0-328-47441-X

2 3 4 5 6 7 8 9 10 V010 18 17 16 15 14 13 12 11 10

Esta es una máquina simple.

Es una palanca.

Ésta es una máquina simple.

Es una rueda.

Ésta es una máquina simple.

Es un eje.

Ésta es una máquina simple.

Es una rampa.

Ésta es una máquina simple.

Es una polea.

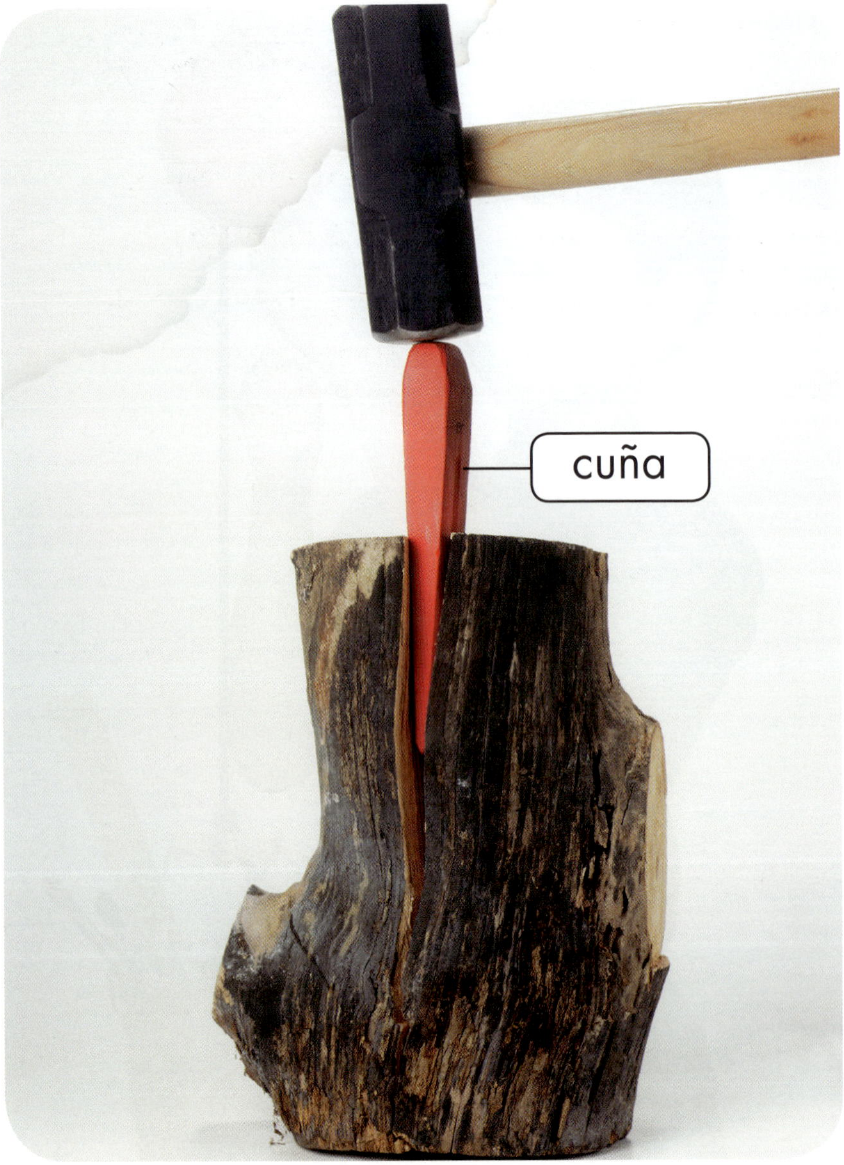

Ésta es una máquina simple.

Es una cuña.